Christ the Healer..

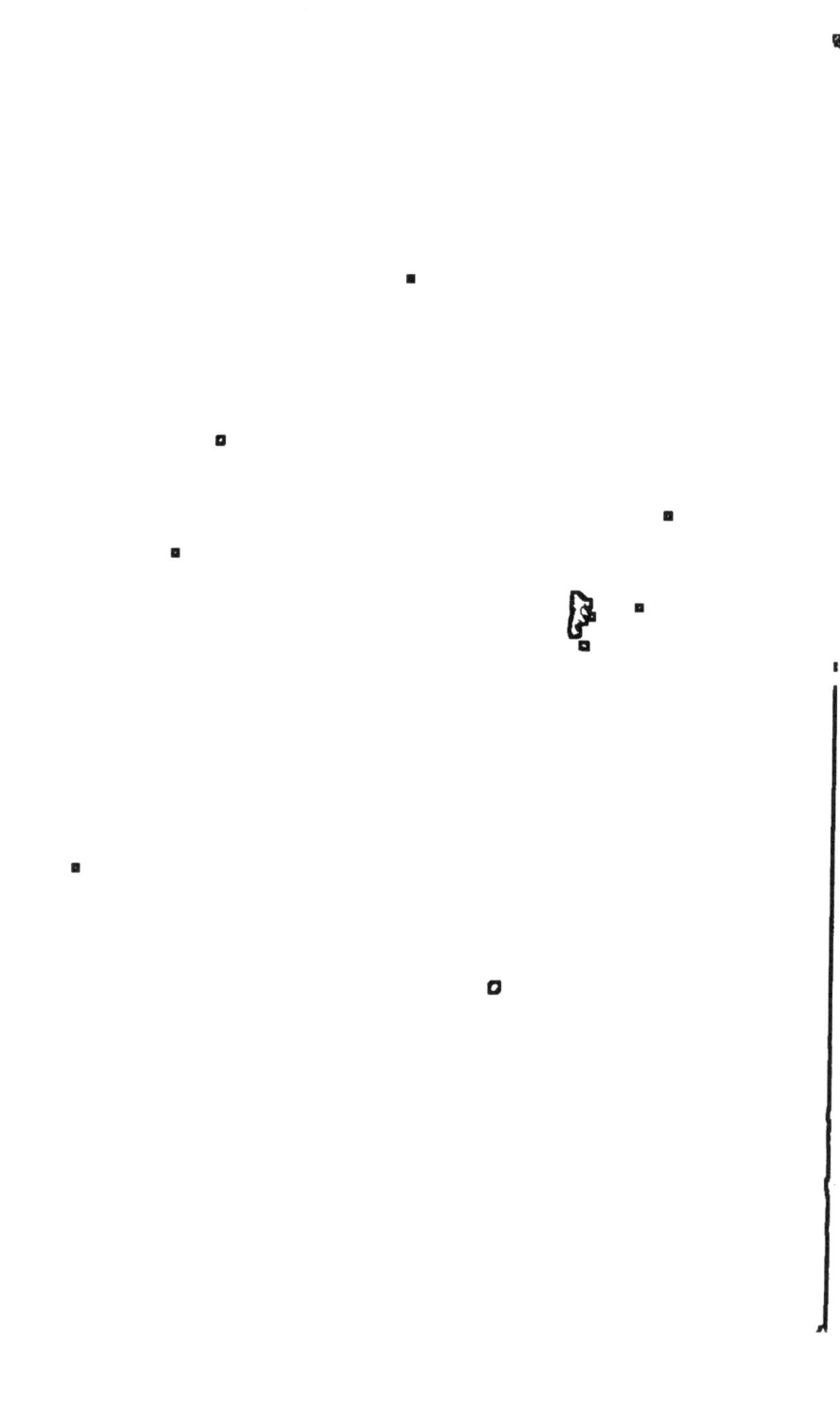

KINGDOM OF GOD.
ONLY BELIEVE.
WHAT IS CHRISTIAN HEALING.

BY

G. F. & M. E. CHAPMAN,

17 HOWARD STREET, - - - MALDEN, MASS.

THREE PAPERS ON PRACTICAL CHRISTIANITY.

ON AND AFTER JANUARY 1ST, 1888,

MRS. M. E. CHAPMAN,

WILL RECEIVE

PATIENTS AT HER RESIDENCE,

17 HOWARD STREET, MALDEN, MASS.

Absent Treatment if desired. All correspondence promptly attended to.

CHRIST THE HEALER.

A SERIES OF

LETTERS ADDRESSED

TO AN

Investigator of Christian Science.

By G. F. CHAPMAN.

BOSTON:
H. H. CARTER & KARRICK,
No. 3 Beacon Street.
1888.

CHRIST THE HEALER.

Dear Friend:

You appear to be very sincere in wishing to find out what true healing is, and I will gladly do all in my power to help you; but the way in which you are trying to learn is so different from the way in which I have been led, that the only aid it is possible for me to give you will come by acquainting you as far as I am able with the revelation which has come to me.

I cannot, if I would, investigate the subject of healing by the light of natural science, as you are trying to do. Such study requires a kind of knowledge that I lack. Nor would the question be really settled, to my thinking, even if the theories of the mental healers should be either established or destroyed by scientific tests; for, if it be *Christian* healing of which the world stands in perishing need, moral as well as physical regeneration, the cure must be wrought by something more powerful than any medicine with which material science deals.

Through trying experiences and sore afflictions have I been led to see that it is the teaching of the Holy Spirit, and not the precepts of worldly wisdom, that brings men to a knowledge of the truth and reveals to them the way of eternal life. "Acquaint yourself with God, whom to know aright is life eternal," is the burden of scripture. "This is life eternal," said our Lord in his memorable prayer, "that they might know thee, the only true God, and Jesus Christ, whom thou hast sent."

The diseases from which men suffer belong not to the body alone, but affect the mind also, and have their source or cause in the wrong beliefs and actions of the human race. The evils of life did not begin when certain bodily maladies first appeared among men; the trouble dates back to that period in the history of mankind called "the Fall." The *Fall* implies a previous state of perfection, and the conclusion seems most reasonable that true healing is accomplished by the redemption of the world through Christ. To answer your question, then, my friend, and solve the problem about which so many people are earnestly thinking, it is necessary to learn what that perfection was from which mankind fell, what the fall itself implies, and what true salvation means.

The only authority on this subject with which I am acquainted is the Bible; and, while I am not wise enough to understand the truth, much less to enlighten you, a deep sense of the meaning of Holy Writ has been given me, which, if I can express it, may enable others to perceive the same glorious light that is shining in upon my once darkened mind.

When Jesus was born in Bethlehem of Judæa, a few wise men from the East saw his star and hastened to worship him as the promised Christ; but most of the people among whom he was brought up failed to recognize his true character. And later, when he went about the villages and highways of Palestine doing the work of him that sent him, his own nation, which he fain would save, rejected his claims and treated him as an imposter. While considering this fact, the question often arises, Does the world, to-day, understand the true Christ any better than the Jews did in the time of Jesus?

The common belief of Christians is that the Saviour of mankind came in the fulness of time in the person of Jesus, the only begotten Son of God, and that men who died before he appeared on earth were saved, if at all, by faith in a *promised* Messiah. Men to-day do not seem to understand, any more than the blind Pharisees did eighteen hundred years ago, that the names "Christ" and "Jesus" stand for two distinct truths that ought not to be confounded. The birth of Jesus, the man, was, indeed, the beginning of the Christian era; but Christ, the only begotten Son of God, was not born of Mary, and dwelt in the bosom of his Father before the human race began, when the morning stars sang together.

On the supposition that Jesus and Christ are identical, the first chapter of the Gospel according to St. John is an unsolved riddle; but, admit the other view, and the sacred words become luminous with a divine meaning. In the beginning, when, as stated in Genesis, God created the heavens and the earth, was the Word, that is, Christ, and the Word was with God, and the Word was God; for Christ declared, " I and my Father are one." All terrestrial things were made by him; life was in him; he was the light that shineth in darkness; he was in the world, and the world was made by him, and the world knew him not. "No man hath seen God at any time," says verse 18th; "the only begotten Son, which is in the bosom of the Father, he hath declared Him."

In my own experience, a new light broke in upon the vexed problems of life when my eyes were opened to perceive the true teaching of the Bible, as I believe, in regard to Christ; and it may surprise you, as it did me at first, to learn that the key to the mystery of Christ is contained in the account of the creation, as given in the first and second chapters of Genesis.

As that account is commonly read and explained, the true sense, as I now understand it, is not made clear. It is usually considered to be descriptive of the first appearance of the visible world of the senses, — of men and beasts, birds and fishes, trees and herbs, as we see them now — and no account is taken of the immaterial substance that constitutes the true prototypes of the forms seen in the natural world.

What is often spoken of as the "Six Days' Creation" I understand to be a presentation of God's idea or pattern of the yet unformed world, as a spiritual reality. By reading the opening verses, we find that God's creation was unlike that which we now behold, for it was *without form and void*. In the beginning it was not visible, for darkness was upon the face of the deep. Nor did it become active until the Spirit of God moved upon the face of this dark abyss. Then, at his command, appeared day and night, dry land, vegetation, sun, moon and stars, fowl of the air, fish of the sea, beasts of the field, and man, made in God's own image. But these were not the external forms of the visible creation, but their spiritual prototypes, the original patterns or models after which the visible things of this world were to be formed. God created the spiritual realities that are represented to our senses in what we call nature, but the realities themselves exist as the spiritual idea of the Creator, without visible form and void of all material qualities.

This may appear at first to be a strained interpretation of the account given in the first chapter of the Old Testament, but is it not the correct one? If the account in the first chapter describes the external creation, how could it be true, as stated in the first verse of the second chapter, that "thus the heavens and the earth were *finished*, and all the host of them?" The external creation did not cease; it is in progress to-day, as we very well know, and has been going on through all the ages in which man has inhabited the earth. It will continue through all time. Generations come and go. Races of men are exterminated, and new races take their place. Earlier forms of animal and plant life become extinct, and other forms spring up in their stead.

The Bible writers speak of the creation as still going on, and the Psalms especially abound with expressions to show that their author considered the creative works of the Lord as continually going forward: The heavens declare the glory of the Lord, and the firmament showeth his handiwork. By the word of the Lord were the heavens made, and all the host of them by the breath of his mouth. He gathereth the waters of the sea together as an heap; he layeth up the depth in storehouses. From the place of his habitation he looketh upon all the inhabitants of the earth. He fashioneth all their hearts alike. Come, behold the works of the Lord, what desolations he hath made in the earth. Which by his strength setteth fast the mountains. Now visitest the earth, and waterest it. How terrible art thou in thy works! Come and see the works of the Lord. He ruleth by his power forever. The Lord is a sun and shield. Oh that men would praise the Lord for his goodness, and for his wonderful works to the children of men. He turneth the wilderness into a standing water, and the dry ground into watersprings. And there he maketh the hungry to dwell. His work is honorable and glorious. The Lord is my strength, and is become my salvation. This is the day which the Lord hath made. Thy hands hath made me and fashioned me. He causeth vapors to ascend from the ends of the earth; he maketh lightnings for the rain; he bringeth the wind out of his treasuries. One generation shall praise thy works to another, and shall declare thy mighty acts. I will speak of the glorious honor of thy majesty, and of thy wondrous works. Thy kingdom is an everlasting kingdom, and thy dominion endureth throughout all generations. The Lord is righteous in all his ways, and holy in all his works. He sendeth forth his commandment upon earth: his word runneth very swiftly. He giveth snow like wool: he scattereth the hoarfrost like ashes. He casteth forth his ice like morsels: who can stand before his cold? He sendeth out his word and melteth them: he causeth his wind to blow, and then waters flow. These and many other familiar passages show, not only that the psalmist considered that the elemental, creative forces operating in nature are the direct will and power of the Lord, but that creation is going on, and is not a finished act.

Nor can we read Psalm cxxxvi. without perceiving that the Lord, to whom the author ascribed all the wonderful works wrought in his time, is the same being who originally created the objects seen in the external world; for he plainly says: O give thanks unto the Lord of lords: . . . To him that by wisdom made the heavens, stretched out the earth above the waters, made great lights — the sun, moon and stars; that smote Egypt, brought out Israel from among them, divided the Red sea, led his people through the wilderness, gave them the land promised to their fathers, and bestowed upon them all the blessings they enjoyed. The same positive truth is also clearly set forth in the verses of Psalm CIV.

From what has been cited, as well as from much other evidence that might be easily adduced, it is certain that the external creation has not come to an end, and that the "heavens and the earth, and all the host of them," that were "finished" when "on the seventh day God ended his work which he had made," must be something else.

Now, I cannot give any learned reasons for what appears to me so plain a truth that no one need miss it, that the Six-Days' Creation was the making of the spiritual prototypes, after which God in his infinite wisdom designed the future visible universe to be fashioned. These existed as his ideas from the beginning; and we, being finite, cannot conceive of a time when they did not exist. When at God's simple word, these spiritual prototypes flashed into being, he pronounced them good, and all being finished, he rested from his work, and left the expression of these ideas or prototypes in external forms to be carried out, as described in the second chapter of the Book of Genesis.

On reading this chapter, we observe that the first three verses record the fact that God had finished the Six-Days' Creation, that he rested on the seventh day, and for that reason that he blessed and sanctified it. Now, mark the peculiarity of the verses that follow. The creating power is designated by a different name. No longer is it God, the Father, who performs the work; but the *Lord God* is thenceforth spoken of as the creator. Up to this time the Lord God had not caused it to rain upon the earth, and there was no man. Why this abrupt change in the appellation of the Creator? And how is the statement that there was not a man to be reconciled with the text of the twenty-seventh verse of the previous chapter, which says: " So God created man in his own image, in the image of God created he him?" Let us consider the last query first.

It appears very plain to me that the creation of man spoken of in the first chapter refers to that spiritual prototype, which is the *real* man and perfect image of God. In the seventh verse of the second chapter it appears that the Lord God gave visible expression to the spiritual model which God had created, by forming a material representation of it "of the dust of the ground." God created a spiritual prototype, the Lord God formed an external resemblance to that model. God created the one perfect image; the Lord God formed a being out of matter, which represented to the senses as far as was possible, the image of God which was its prototype.

The query, "Why this abrupt change in the appellation of the Creator?" is answered, if we accept the truth of the statement that God had already finished his creative work, and that the forming of the external or visible creation was and still is a work carried on by the Lord. By this it is not meant that a totally different power assumed and carried forward the work of creation, for that would imply the existence of more than one deity. The name Lord God, and the name Lord, as frequently used throughout the Bible, refer to the spiritual likeness of God, the account of which is given in verses 26–7, of chapter first, where it is called man.

When God said " Let us make man in our image," it was not the first specimen of the corporeal, earthly man that was created; this "image of God" was God's *ideal* man, the spiritual prototype, of which each individual of the race is the physical expression. This was the *real* and *perfect* man, to whom power was given to people the earth with corporeal beings to represent him, and all varieties of animal and vegetable life, formed after God's idea.

Again, this perfect image of the Father was *God's only begotten son*, existing from the beginning, whose prerogative it was to create all lower orders of terrestrial life. He is the Lord, who made the heavens and the earth, the sea, and all that in them is.

He is the Lord, who appeared as Christ, in the person of Jesus of Nazareth, and became the savior of the world.

The creation of the spiritual prototypes had been finished, and a new mode of the divine creative power was manifested as the Lord God, maker of the forms of the visible or external world. In the Psalms he is called "the Lord, our maker," the Lord who "made the heavens and the earth." "It is he that hath made us and not we ourselves."— Psalms c., 3. "Who laid the foundations of the earth, that it should not be removed forever."— CIV., 5. "The works of the Lord are great, sought out of all them that have pleasure therein."— CXI., 2. "Let them praise the name of the Lord: for he commanded, and they were created."— CXLVIII., 5.

Paul's testimony on this point, as given in the first chapter of Hebrews, and elsewhere, is very clear. The meaning is plain that the Lord, who in the beginning laid the foundation of the earth, is the only begotten Son of God, whose throne is for ever and ever. Still further is this view confimed if we now compare chapter v., 5 : " So also Christ glorified not himself to be made an high priest; but he that said unto him, Thou art my Son, to-day have I begotten thee." In Colossians I., the same apostle reiterates this view ; for he says " Who [the Son] is the image of the invisible God, the first-born of every creature : For by him were all things created, that are in heaven, and that are in earth, . . . And he is before all things, and by him all things consist."—Verses 15-17. In this connection read also II. Corinthians IV., 4 : " Lest the light of the glorious gospel of Christ, who is the image of God, should shine unto them." I. Corinthians, x., 4, 9 : " And did all drink the same spiritual drink : for they drank of that spiritual Rock that followed them: and that Rock was Christ." "Neither let us tempt Christ, as some of them also tempted, and were destroyed of serpents." Acts VII., 37, 38 : "This [Christ] is that Moses, which said unto the children of Israel, A prophet shall the Lord your God raise up unto you of your brethren, like unto me; him shall ye hear. This is he that was in the church in the wilderness with the angel which spake to him in the mount Sina, and with our fathers: who received the lively oracles to give unto us." Colossians I., 18: "And he is the head of the body, the church: who is the beginning, the first-born from the dead; that in all things he might have the pre-eminence." Ephesians IV., 12, 13: "For the edifying of the *body* of Christ: Till we all come in the unity of the faith, and of the knowledge of the Son of God, unto a perfect man, unto the measure of the stature of the fulness of Christ." John I., 1, 14, 18: "In the beginning was the Word" [Christ]. "And the Word was made flesh, and dwelt among us, (and we beheld his glory, the glory as of the only begotten of the Father,) full of grace and truth." "No man hath seen God at any time; the only begotten Son, which is in the bosom of the Father, he hath declared him." John III., 35: "The Father loveth the Son, and hath given all things into his hand." John VIII., 58: "Jesus said unto them, Verily, verily, I say unto you, Before Abraham was, I am." John XVII., 5: "And now, O Father, glorify thou me, with thine own self with the glory which I had with thee before the world was." Matthew XXII., 45: "If David then call him Lord, how is he his son?" Matthew XVI., 16: "Thou art the Christ, the son of the living God." Mark VIII., 29: "Thou art the Christ."

THE FALL.

If the correct interpretation of the many texts now cited make it evident that Christ, the only begotten son of God, existing from the beginning, is the creator of the external world, as declared in the second chapter of Genesis, you will find it easy to perceive that this only begotten Son is the one spiritual or real man, of which the race of corporeal men are the visible expressions.

To perceive this is very important; for when we realize that there is only one real man, who is the spiritual prototype, having power to form an indefinite number of material expressions of himself, we can better understand how it is that the *real man* is perfect, and cannot be affected by what is called disease and sin. We see also that it is through Christ, as a perfect prototype, that we have any idea at all of divine perfection.

And lest my use of the term "corporeal man" lead any one astray, let me explain that by it I intend to designate an individual of the human race on earth, with all that belongs to him as a personality; not his physical body alone, but his soul as well; and my reason for calling this creature a "corporeal man" is merely to distinguish the external expression of the one real man from the prototype itself.

Adam and Eve were the perfect outward or material expression of the one real or spiritual man, who was created male and female; for the Lord God "breathed into his nostrils the breath of life, and man became a living soul." But it was not Adam who exercised dominion over all the lower orders of creation. He was what the Hebrew meaning of the word implies, the *earth man*, that is, the earthly or visible expression of man. He had no life of himself, but derived his life from the breath of his creator, the spiritual man. He could do nothing of himself, but was the external organ through which the power of the real man was made manifest on the earth.

THE FALL. 25

The same truth is taught in the parable of the Vine and the Branches, recorded in the fifteenth chapter of the Gospel of John. Christ, the spiritual man, is the true vine, the Father is the husbandman, and external or corporeal human beings are the branches. How forcibly does Jesus here teach the lesson that the external man has no life or power in himself, but is wholly dependent on the vine. He is simply the outward expression of the spiritual man, and is created only as a medium through which the spiritual will expresses itself.

We see, also, that it was not the spiritual man that fell, but the corporeal man. The lapse of Adam, or the earth-man, from a state of perfect innocence represented in Genesis as expulsion from the garden of Eden, took place when the branches were broken off from the vine, and the external was no longer a true expression of the spiritual or real. How this fall came about is explained in Romans i., 21–25: "Because that, when they knew God, they glorified him not as God, neither were thankful; but became vain in their imaginations, and their foolish heart was darkened. Professing themselves to be wise, they became fools, and changed the glory of the uncorruptible God into an image made like to corruptible man, and to birds, and four-footed beasts, and creeping things. Wherefore God also gave them up to uncleanness through the lusts of their own hearts, to dishonor their own bodies between themselves: who changed the truth of God into a lie, and worshiped and served the creature [corporeal man] more than the creator [spiritual man], who is blessed for ever."

When the fallen man realized in a measure his true condition and began once more to turn his gaze toward the Vine, or true light, the question naturally arose, Where am I? But to his darkened mind it seemed like the voice of God calling to him, and saying, "Adam, where art thou?" With this came the knowledge that he was separated in thought from the spiritual source of life, and hence was generated the fear of danger; and he sought to cover himself from the light which revealed the fact of his disobedience.

The sign that man had fallen was that he came to know good from evil; for we read in Genesis III., 5: "For God doth know that in the day ye eat thereof [*i. e.*, of the forbidden tree], then your eyes shall be opened, and ye shall be as gods, knowing good and evil." As if the tempter had said: After eating that fruit, ye, who are now simply the corporeal external expressions and mediums of the Lord, shall become to yourselves what ye now think God is.

Is it not remarkable, also, that the knowledge they were forbidden to acquire, is the very knowledge which the Christian churches now think it most needful for men to have? Great emphasis is laid on the cultivation of a tender conscience, that is quick to distinguish what is right from what is wrong. But the Lord God said to our first parents: "Of the tree of the knowledge of good and evil, *thou shalt not eat:* for in the day that thou eatest thereof *thou shalt surely die.*"

If that assertion was true then, it is true to-day, and will be always true. What then are we to infer, but that the knowledge of good and evil, that is the power to discriminate between what is right and what is wrong is the sign that men are smitten with spiritual death? Or, in other words, the branches have ceased to abide in the vine from which alone they could draw their life?

The condition of perfect innocence and delight, called the garden of Eden, was one in which the inmates knew nothing but good (God). The original sin was finding out that a man may indulge thoughts and feelings that are not good; and when a man has made that discovery, he is fallen. "Sin, when it is finished bringeth forth death," said the apostle; a statement which tallies exactly with those awful words uttered by the Lord God: "In the day that thou eatest thereof thou shalt surely die."

The fatal thought that a man might have power of himself apart from the Lord, that he might sever himself from the vine, and become a god unto himself, and know of his own knowledge what was right and what wrong, instead of relying wholly on the Lord for guidance, is represented in Genesis as being put into the minds of Adam and Eve by a serpent. It was, therefore, from the lowest "beast of the field," the most earthy and material source that this fatal ambition sprung. Man turned away from the light to the darkness; ceased to look upward, and began to look downward; "changed the glory of the uncorruptible God into an image made like to corruptible man."

The desire to put a personal will in place of God's will, to act for ourselves and exercise our own judgment, instead of being glad, obedient mediums through which the Lord may work, is called in the Bible a serpent,—a sensual, earth-born suggestion. When the children of Israel had sinned while on their journey in the wilderness, they died of serpent bites; and, curiously enough, they were saved from the deadly effects of the poison of sin, by the lifting up of the brazen type of the destroyer, thereby directing the eyes and thoughts of the dying sinners toward the true source of life.

Thus is the lesson taught over and over, in the blessed Word of God, that as soon as the corporeal man learns to know both good and evil, he dies of the serpent-bite of sin; and it is only when he forsakes that desire to judge for himself what is right and wrong, and yields himself wholly to the guidance of the perfect man, Christ, that he is saved.

THE SAVIORS OF THE WORLD.

I have explained to you what the Bible means by Christ, as I understand it,—that Christ is the only begotten Son of the Father, and the Lord God mentioned in the second chapter of Genesis; he is the real man and spiritual prototype of all corporeal beings belonging to the human race on earth, and the creator of everything finite. I have also considered the teaching of Scripture concerning the fall of man, which was a lapse from rectitude and consequent innocence, induced by the desire to take his life into his own hands, constitute himself a judge of good and evil, and draw his life from the earth, instead of abiding in the vine. From this lapsed and dying condition fallen men could be rescued only by infinite power; hence the next subject to be treated is the Saviors of the World.

According to my present understanding of truth, Christ, who was made flesh and dwelt among men in the person of Jesus of Nazareth, also appears in every individual human being. Each babe that is born is a new outward expression of the Christ, a visible medium, more or less perfect, through which he manifests himself to the world. Not one is so obscure or degenerate, that he does not in some degree reflect the image of this perfect prototype; for no one comes into this world absolutely devoid of goodness, and whatever is good proceeds from the Lord, who is striving to manifest himself through every earthly expression he has made.

It is true that the children of men, spoken of in the parable as the "branches," do not abide in the vine, and consequently fail to bear fruit. We see painful evidence on every hand that men have turned the truth of God into a lie and serve the creature more than the creator. Yet these unfruitful branches are not wholly severed from the vine from which they derive their life; for, if they were indeed cut off, they would be cast forth and withered, as Jesus said; there would then be nothing to sustain spiritual, or even what is called physical life, and the severed branches would utterly perish. But the fact that the wicked continue to live and enjoy God's bounty proves that every earthly life, however dark, has some vital connection with the divine life which nourishes it.

All men are expressions of the one spiritual prototype, better or worse mediums of Christ on the earth. And just so far as he is a clear medium for spiritual truth to shine through is each man a savior of those who come within his influence. It is Christ, the truth, pervading the dark world, and operating in the human heart, that redeems and saves the race; and wherever there is a medium through which the light of truth can shine, be it never so faintly, there is a source of healing and saving grace to mankind.

The most perfect expression of the real man, that is, the Christ, of which we have any knowledge, was seen in the person of Jesus. He was *the* savior of mankind. But there were men living before his time through whom the Christ manifested himself to the world in a special manner, and just such men have lived since his advent. All human beings are saviors, in so far as they reflect that perfect image and likeness of the Father, which is Christ, the spiritual man; but each age has had its saviors, men endued with a double portion of the Christ spirit, and of some of these we will now speak.

One of the earliest saviors mentioned in the Bible is Noah, who appeared on earth after the race of men had become very wicked, so that, as we read in Genesis vi., 5: "every imagination of the thoughts of his heart was only evil continually." But Noah found grace in the eyes of the Lord, because "he was a just man, perfect in his generation, and walked with God." The account of his life and deeds given in Genesis clearly indicates that through him the outward human expression of the Christ was preserved from utter extinction on earth. With him the Lord renewed the covenant formerly made with Adam; and through him the branches became once more united to the vine.

Noah understood, as the people about him did not, the spiritual condition of the world, and that it was the gross sins of those who had forgotten God that were surely bringing about their ruin. He saw too that the only salvation for the branches was in an unbroken union with the true vine, which was Christ, the Lord. Thus through his knowledge of the truth and obedience thereto were some branches saved and reunited to the vine, while many perished, because they had severed their connection with the only source of spiritual life.

Abraham, the faithful, was in a special sense a savior to the people of his day. The people of the land and his own kindred had made to themselves gods in the likeness of things earthly, and were wholly given over to idolatry, so that they no longer understood the true source of their life. But Abraham still preserved conscious communion with the God of his fathers, and lived according to the light of truth. He was, therefore, bidden to separate himself from his kindred, and, emigrating to another land, established there the true worship of God, and a purer way of life, that should be a pattern to all mankind.

The manner in which Abraham is spoken of in Genesis is peculiar, and not easily explained except on the assumption that he was indeed a savior of the people of his time in a special sense. We read that the Lord made a covenant with him, and promised, as recorded in the twelfth chapter, to bless him in a signal manner, and make of him a great nation. The third verse of this chapter contains language not unlike that applied to Jesus himself; for the Lord said to Abraham, "I will bless them that bless thee, and curse him that curseth thee: *and in thee shall all the families of the earth be blessed.*" So also, in the eighteenth chapter, eighteenth verse: "Seeing that Abraham shall surely become a great and mighty nation, *and all the nations of the earth shall be blessed in him.*"

One cannot read attentively the biblical account of the life and acts of this first of Hebrew patriarchs without perceiving that in him was preserved among his people a knowledge of God, and he was to them a mediator, as in the case of the doomed inhabitants of Sodom and Gomorrah, for whom he prayed. In like manner were Isaac, Jacob, and Joseph, lineal descendants and successors of Abraham, singled out from their contemporaries, to be in a special sense the saviors of their times. The blessing and covenant of the Lord were with them; the Christ found visible expression through them more than through any others of their day; and through them signal blessings were transmitted to all who came within the circle of their influence.

It is true that, in the Bible accounts of these worthies, we do not see evidence that in them bodily, as in the person of Jesus, "dwelt all the fulness of the godhead." Of none of them can it be said, "He was tempted in all points like as we are, *yet without sin.*" The Christ found only a partial, not a perfect expression through their lives; and as mediums of the truth they did not attain the lofty standard revealed to the human race in Jesus, the perfect savior, which was for to come.

Moses, the great Hebrew leader and lawgiver, was a savior of his people in a higher and better sense than any who had preceded him in the history of mankind. His advent on earth resembled that of Jesus in many important particulars. He is first introduced to us as a humble, helpless babe, whose life, like that of the babe of Bethlehem, was put in jeopardy by the edict of a cruel tyrant. The years of his early manhood were passed in obscurity, as were those of Jesus. The Lord manifested his presence to Moses by a flame of fire in a bush, as he subsequently did to the man Jesus, in the form of a dove. In each case there was heard a voice of assurance. Moses talked with the unseen Christ in the cloud-capped mountain of Sinai; Jesus held a similar interview in the mount of transfiguration. The former wrought signs and wonders in Egypt, as proof of his high authority; the latter did the same thing when he appeared and taught in Palestine. Moses uttered the Decalogue; Jesus fulfilled it with a profounder meaning. Moses delivered his people from bondage, and established them under a new dispensation and a code of laws sanctioned by the Most High; Jesus delivered them out of bondage to the letter of these laws, and revived in them the true spirit of obedience, under the gospel dispensation. Moses was sent by the Lord, as a special manifestation, or material appearance of himself, to the chosen people, just as Jesus was sent in a later age; for, in Exodus III., 10, we read: "Come now therefore, I will send thee unto Pharaoh, that thou mayest bring forth my people the children of Israel out of Egypt."

That the Lord, or Christ, did indeed appear in the person of Moses, as a special savior of his people seems evident from the text of the song. in which Moses explains, in a condensed form, the spiritual condition of the children of Israel to whom he was sent. This song may be found in Deuteronomy xxxii., from which the following verses are taken:

"Because I will publish the name of the Lord: ascribe ye greatness unto our God.

"He is a Rock, his work is perfect: for all his ways are judgment: a God of truth and without iniquity, just and right is he.

"Do ye thus requite the Lord, O foolish people and unwise? Is he not thy father that hath bought thee? hath he not made thee, and established thee?

" * * * Then he forsook God which made him, and lightly esteemed the Rock of his salvation.

"They provoked him to jealousy with strange gods, with abominations provoked they him to anger.

"Of the Rock that begat thee thou art unmindful, and hast forgotten God that formed thee.

"For their rock is not as our Rock, even our enemies themselves being judges.

"For the Lord shall judge his people, and repent himself for his servants, when he seeth that their power is gone, and there is none shut up, or left.

"See now that I, even I, am he, and there is no god with me: I kill, and I make alive; I wound and I heal; neither is there any that can deliver out of my hand."

There is warrant also for believing that the Hebrew nation produced no savior equal to Moses, until the advent of Jesus himself; for, in the tenth verse of the last chapter of Deuteronomy, it is recorded that "there arose not a prophet since in Israel like unto Moses, whom the Lord knew face to face."

From the time of Moses until the advent of Jesus the Jewish nation had a long succession of special saviors, known as judges and prophets, on whom Christ impressed a double portion of his spirit, and through whom he manifested himself to his people, calling them back to God the Father, and reuniting them to himself, the true vine. Conspicuous among these leaders and saviors of the children of Israel were Joshua, the successor of Moses; Samson, upon whom, it is recorded in Judges, the spirit of the Lord came mightily at times; Samuel, who was dedicated by his mother to the service of the Lord; David, the anointed king and sweet singer of Israel; Elijah, Elisha, and Isaiah, prophets of the Lord, Ezra, the scribe; and a long line of worthies, who kept the law and held to the worship of the true God, in a land given over to idolatry and evil.

THE CHRIST IN JESUS.

Thus far my letters have had reference to the appearance of the Christ during the earlier and prophetic ages of the world's history, ages in which the most perfect mediums reflected but dimly the central light of truth, which is the life of the human race. Yet it seems to me that no prayerful student of the Scriptures can fail to discern the evidence that the long line of righteous men mentioned in the Bible, in so far as they acted under the direction of the Lord, were earthly expressions and mediums through which Christ, the true vine, revealed himself.

Now, therefore, we may turn our attention to that brightest of all manifestations of the one only begotten Son, in Jesus of Nazareth; he who came in the form of a servant of the lowest, that he might redeem and save a world lying in darkness and in the shadow of death.

Much might be said, did the object of this writing demand it, on the peculiar significance of the birth and child-life of this wonderful being, who, even at the tender age of twelve years, began to speak as never man spake. But, since it is rather with his career and mission as a teacher of truth that we have to do, I will pass this topic; merely remarking that, it seems to me that, only by appearing among men in the humble, yet apparently miraculous manner in which he did, could he have illustrated to his own nation and to the world the true idea of Christ the life of men, redeeming the world unto himself.

At the time of the advent of Jesus, the Jews as a nation had lost the divine sense of the presence and power of the true God of their fathers, and were paying outward, formal worship to a deity fashioned after their own material and vain imaginations. Jesus came to announce a gospel of good tidings, and reveal to them, in place of what they ignorantly called God, that Christ who was the express image of the Father (true

God), and the Spirit of life. He came to show them the true relation between the vine and the branches, and to verify the words, "Whosoever seeth me seeth the Father also."

When John, the forerunner of Jesus, announced him as "he, who, coming after me, is preferred before me;" as "the Lamb of God, who taketh away the sins of the world;" he, whose shoe-latchet the Baptist was unworthy to loose; he discerned in Jesus the most perfect expression and medium of the Christ, which had ever been sent among men. John well knew that he himself was not that Light; but he testified that Jesus, about whom men were curiously speculating, was the true Light, which lighteth every man that cometh into the world. The burden of his testimony and the claim of Jesus himself was, that he came into the world to restore to a race which had lost it a knowledge of the true source of their life; to assure them that the corporeal man with his external ceremonies and cares was not the *real* man; that the

God, whom they so punctiliously worshipped and sacrificed to in consecrated cities and places, was not the true God, who requires a spiritual worship and needs no temples or dwelling-place.

Jesus came to show men how to rise into the true life by vital union with Christ the true vine; he also illustrated to them, both by teaching and by example, the power of such a life upon the body of man. Both Jesus and John were confirmed in their belief concerning the mission of the former on earth by what sounded to them as the voice of Christ himself saying, "This is my beloved son, in whom I am well pleased;" that is: "This Jesus is a man who is to be so pure a medium for truth, that through him I am pleased to manifest myself as the light and life of the world most fully." Henceforth all that men needed to do was to admit the light into the dark recesses of their worldly minds, and as John declared, make a straight path through the wilderness of their own evil, material thoughts for the entrance of the Lord's truth.

Take notice, also, that before entering upon his work as a teacher of men, Jesus descended into this wilderness of common or material thought, that he might contemplate life in its unrenewed phases, and by fasting and prayer, overcome the temptations that lead men astray through the devil of selfhood. Here the man Jesus learned the important lessons that true life is derived from God, and man must live in the spirit, not by bread alone; that man has no right to presume on divine protection to enable him to carry out purely selfish and earth-born desires, for that is tempting the Lord; that it is not for a man to seek dominion and authority in this world, but to serve the Lord by becoming a clear medium of the truth.

Having thus tested the power of worldly ambition and the tempter, and become persuaded that there is no life for man except that derived from Spirit, Jesus went forth to preach to men, and let the Christ light shine through him. "And Jesus went about all Galilee, teaching in their synagogues, and preaching the gospel of the kingdom, and healing all manner of sickness and all manner of disease among the people."— Matthew IV., 23.

The next wonderful thing in the life of Jesus was that, when he had overcome the temptations of his lower self, so that the union between Jesus the man and Christ the Lord became close and vital, so much of the spirit of Christ was reflected in him, that the sick felt the life-giving virtue, and were healed. We do not read that Jesus studied "Christian science" or any other form of mental healing, or that he sought to learn the art of Eastern theosophists and Hebrew cabalists. The inference is so plain that it seems impossible to miss it, that while Jesus was doing the work he came into the world to perform, even while he was preaching the gospel of the kingdom of Christ his father, and calling upon men everywhere to repent, there went out from his sacred person an involuntary influence which healed the sick with whom he came in contact. He was a healer of the soul; but the cure of the infirmities of the flesh followed as a matter of course. He healed men of whatsoever diseases they had, not by *science*, for he had none; but the wholeness of the Christ-life pervading the minds and hearts of those who listened to his divine words, filled them with a new sense of life, that made them whole.

So clear was the evidence of this fact, that observers like Nicodemus, exclaimed, "We know thou art a teacher come from God: for no man can do the wonderful works which thou doest, except the spirit of God work through him."

It is impossible to conceive how a man, charged with the mission of saving the world and reuniting mankind to the spiritual source of all life, could consent to lay aside his father's business, while he vied with the physicians and magicians in curing the bodily ailments of the people who flocked about him. It was spiritual wholeness which he sought,— a wholeness that included health to the body, but never produced the latter and least important, without working the greater transformation typified by the "new birth."

It is only on such a supposition that Jesus could have dismissed the messengers sent by John to inquire who he was, with the answer, "Go your way, and tell John what things ye have seen and heard; how that the blind see, the lame walk, the lepers are cleansed, the deaf hear, the dead are raised, to the poor the gospel is preached."

And how is the spiritual sense of the beatitudes and precepts contained in the Sermon on the Mount to be made apparent, until we perceive that Jesus was impressing the Mosaic law, the letter of which his hearers blindly observed, with a new interior life? "Let your light so shine before men," he said, "that they may see your good works, and glorify your Father which is in heaven;" that is to say: Let the Father's glory — the Christ spirit — be so manifest in your works or conduct, that those who behold you may perceive that your goodness is the life of the Lord shining through you.

The miracles of Jesus were instances of the visible manifestation of spiritual power, that appealed very forcibly to the material thought of those who witnessed them. When they saw water turned into wine, a multitude fed in the desert with a supply of food scarcely sufficient to give each a little morsel, a great draught of fishes taken where men had fished all night without taking any, they could not help believing that he who had power to produce such results in the natural world possessed indeed a spirit of which they did not know.

In this connection, I wish to assert my belief that there is a spiritual condition, not well understood, but which it is possible for men to attain, whereby they may exercise a power over nature and the things of the external world. He, who was creator of everything finite, might easily exercise that creative force in such a way as to produce a given effect at any time. It surely could not be impossible for Christ, the Lord, who created the heavens and the earth, the sea, and all that in them is, to work the change whereby the water became wine, a few loaves were multiplied into a bountiful supply of bread, and a school of fish were collected in a particular locality. Jesus was so filled with this power of Christ, that such acts were easy to him; and I cannot help thinking that it is possible for any one to do like wonderful works, who is a clear medium of spiritual power.

But while Jesus occasionally displayed such power over the elements of nature, he still taught the people that such physical good was not the highest end to be sought. He showed them that it was not the water or wine drunk to quench bodily thirst, but the water of life that men should crave, which, if once tasted, would prevent the return of thirst; for it would be in them, a well of water springing up unto everlasting life. He bade his followers seek not the bread which perisheth, but the true bread of life, of which, if a man eat he shall never die. And further, he declared that he, the Christ speaking to them through his corporeal lips, is that bread of life. "Labor not for the meat which perisheth," were his words, " but for that meat which endureth unto everlasting life."

Another very important feature of the

teachings of Jesus is his doctrine concerning death and the resurrection. He was surrounded by those who held that, at the death of the body, the soul or ghost departed to sheol, or the under world, there to tarry for an indefinite period, until a final judgment day; those who accepted the belief in Hades, borrowed from the Greeks and Romans; those who believed like the Egyptians that, after death, the soul passes onward through a long cycle of changes, till it reaches the awful tribunal of Osiris, the chief of the Egyptian deities; those who, like the Saducees, professed to believe in annihilation, and that physical death ends all. To all these people Jesus declared a new doctrine of life, and put a new meaning on what they called death.

It was to these people that Jesus said: "Verily, verily, I say unto you, if a man keep my sayings, he shall never see death." "Whosoever liveth and believeth in me shall never die." "I am the resurrection and the life." To listeners holding the common notions about death such words must have sounded strangely; and yet, how is it possible to avoid the conclusion that he who uttered them, was not speaking of that change which comes at last to every human body? More sayings are in accord with the declaration of Paul, that, "as in Adam all died, even so, in Christ shall all be made alive;" and with that other utterance of Jesus: "He that saveth his life shall lose it; but he that loseth his life for my sake shall find it."

The doctrine of the resurrection announced by the Master, while he stood with the mourners at the tomb of Lazarus, does not seem to me to have any reference to the revivifying of the body. The death he referred to, and out of which he was able to raise mankind, was that spiritual condition into which men come who sever themselves in thought and belief from the true soucre of life, and live as of themselves. He came to revive in the soul the sense of dependence on Christ for spiritual life, to unite the broken branches to the vine; hence he could say with the utmost propriety, " I am the resurrection and the life." His mission was through the power of living truth to raise men out of that state of spiritual apathy, in which they had lost vital connection with the true vine, and restore to them *real* life, by making them conscious of that interior change, which he elsewhere called the "new birth." What he taught was that, until men lose their lives, that is, part with selfishness, they cannot save their lives spiritually. For all *real* life is derived from the Lord; and when a man comes to understand and believe this, " even though he were dead, yet shall he live."

THE HEALING CHRIST.

What I now have to write, in reply to your last questions, bears directly on the subject of mental or Christian healing, about which you are so anxious to learn. It has taken some time to reach this point; but, believing as I firmly do, that true healing cannot be understood until the Bible doctrine concerning Christ is clearly apprehended, I have tried to expound it to you, as it has been shown me, in order to have a sure foundation upon which to base a theory of those remarkable cures, which are puzzling so many curious people to-day.

As I have already intimated, it seems evident to me that healing, as practised by Jesus, began with a spiritual renovation, and ended by producing moral, then mental, and, finally, physical wholeness. In such cures the steps of the process follow each other in natural order; for the stream is first purified at its source, and then the healing waters carry life and soundness to every part. There may be a bodily change, called a *cure*, that begins and ends with the material; but it is not what Jesus meant when he asked a sufferer, "Wouldst thou be made whole?" He taught that it was the truth that made men free; free from sin, free from fear of harm, free from the bodily ailments consequent on sin and fear. Wholeness was the result of abiding in the vine, a most natural instance of cause and effect.

I am not one of those who hold that the earthly mission of Jesus was to be a doctor, and go about curing bodily diseases. What happened to those who came under his treatment was only the natural experience of a saved soul; their sicknesses being the results of sin, of turning away from the Christ-life, when they repented and were reunited to the true vine, a thorough healing could not but result. I do not believe that a man is saved until he is free from sin,— I do not believe he is saved until he is free from bodily disease; but I believe that the last result follows naturally from the first.

Jesus, when on earth, worked his cures without the use of visible means of the nature of medicines. He also enjoined it upon his disciples and apostles to heal the sick in the same way; and we find that, after his departure, the same power came to them, or acted through them, for they, too, healed, by invoking the name of their master.

But while working in this wonderful way themselves, Jesus and his disciples did not condemn the use of other means. They did not need to employ or recommend material agents; but there is no record of their condemning the use of drugs and mechanical means of helping the sick, because they in their treatment were able to dispense with all these. And the lesson plainly taught us is that, if we have reached a condition in which we do not need the presence of a material remedy, to change the thought in sickness, but can safely rely on the direct operation upon the mind of spiritual forces, we should praise God for this, and pray constantly that our lives may so reflect the truth that has mercifully been made plain to us, that our brother man may take knowledge of us that we have indeed been with Christ, and be led to glorify God also.

Nor should we scorn the services of an honest physician or nurse, because we seem no longer to need them. When they administer a medicine to change the thought of the sick, the same power that healed those who sought to be made whole by the Savior brings health to their patients. Medical men may sometimes have mistaken the true province of the remedies they administered, but we have no reason to doubt that they have been the means of an untold amount of good in the past, and will be needed for years to come. It will certainly be a long time before the majority of men will come to believe that the diseases from which they suffer can be cured by any other than physical or medicinal agencies.

But new light on this subject may come to an honest doctor, as well as to the non-professional; he may be led to see that it is not his medicine that heals, and that it is possible to dispense with material means, and produce even better results. A case in point comes to mind. Not long ago a well known physician, while riding about among his patients, became greatly absorbed in the problem of what, after all, it is that restores health. He knew that the power was not in the drugs; he felt that it was not in the physician;— What then cured the patients? and how were the sick restored when under the care of so-called Christian healers? He pondered the subject long and anxiously; and at length it came into his mind that it was "the love of God in the heart" that cured the sick. Nor did he reason unwisely; for surely we are taught that it is the love of God in the heart that casteth out all fear.

The doctor had solved the question, and found the secret of health. The love of God, which passeth all understanding of material thought, casteth out all fear; and since fear is the parent of disease, sickness disappears when that is cast out, or destroyed. This perfect love is the motive power in the world to-day, working throughout the universe, changing, cleansing, and healing the soul.

I am often asked how it is that I heal. But I do not believe there is a living being on earth who can explain in a satisfactory manner how this wonderful healing is done. Mental healers generally consider that the power comes to those who study into and accept the peculiar teachings known as "Christian science," and forms akin to that. But to this view of the case I do not assent; and, in order to make my own position clear, I will give you somewhat in detail my own experience.

Before attempting this, however, allow me to record my conviction that there is good in all forms of healing, in which it is the earnest wish of the operator to help the sick by leading them to turn away from mere bodily troubles and material remedies, to the one only source of genuine healing power. Hence there should be a spirit of unity and love and not of antagonism between them. And, in fact, the best evidence, and the only evidence that they are working in the spirit of Christ, that is, are filled with and controlled by his spirit, is that they entertain a cordial love for each other, and seek each other's good as well as each his own. If a person who practises mental healing according to one particular method which he has learned treats all who follow different ways of healing as malpractitioners and evil doers, he surely fails to furnish the best and most reliable proof that he is himself actuated by the spirit of Christ; and if he calls his own method *Christian* healing, and condemns all others as unchristian, no good people who understand this will believe that he really belongs to the fold of Christ.

The possibility of a mental cure or faith-healing is believed in by the church in which I was educated, and I did some very satisfactory work of that kind before I made a special study of any special way of using the art. Later I took a course of lessons in what is called "Christian science." It seemed to me, after getting somewhat acquainted with people of this way of healing, that they have gotten hold of one side of a great truth, which is grasped more or less firmly; and in the class I joined there were honest seekers after truth, who were led as I was to attend the course of instruction given by the "Christian science" teacher, hoping to receive important spiritual help.

The lessons consisted of a series of twelve talks by the teacher, on subjects presented in the following order: First, their doctrine concerning God; second, concerning mind; third, concerning matter. We were told, in substance, that God is one; principle, and not a person; life, truth, and love; the only intelligence and substance in the universe. God is omnipotent, omniscient, and omnipresent; hence he fills all space, is all, and there is nothing else but God. Moreover, God is perfectly good; hence there can be no such thing as evil; and if there is no evil, sin, sickness, and death, which are the consequences or effects of evil, have no reality.

Having assumed what had been asserted concerning God as proved and accepted, the teacher proceeded to argue that all that God created must be like himself, perfect and spiritual. The world, therefore, which is the creation of God, and all living creatures are like him, and must be spiritual. Hence all is mind or idea; and nothing else can be real. To put the case in other words, mind is the only reality, and what men call matter is a delusion, a false belief. There is really no such thing as a body, a tree, a flower, a landscape, a sheet of water, or, in fact, anything that we are wont to call material.

Of course, the body being unreal, it was easy to assume that the bodily ailments, called disease, cannot be real; and, since " God is of purer eyes than to behold iniquity," and human beings are created in his perfect image, there can be no such thing as sin and consequent death. Such being the case, one has only to hold these facts firmly in mind, in order to heal the sick.

But plain as this theory of the world appeared to the teacher of " Christian science," I was not so thoroughly convinced but that a number of troublesome questions arose in my mind. " If all sin and pain and death be unreal and a delusion," I asked, what is it that is forever struggling with the delusion, and trying to get free from the effects of a wrong belief?" The answer was, "There is no one struggling or trying to get free; it is simply a dream or imagination." "Then who is the dreamer?" I asked, still more perplexed. "There is no dreamer," replied the confident teacher; and I was not disposed to press the matter any further.

There are many things insisted on as true by those who profess to believe "Christian science" which it is not easy to put faith in. Much must be assumed on the authority of some person's assertion, for which no satisfactory reason is given and no sanction is to be found in Scripture. They affirm that there is no evil, no sickness, no death; our belief that such conditions exist is only a dream of a dreamer who has no reality; all is God; all is good; all is perfect; all is harmonious; you are not sick; you have no pain; and this work of healing many consider the most important work in which a human being can engage.

I would by no means imply that " Christian scientists" are not sincere in their belief, or that a theory that appears so absurd to others does not seem correct to them. It does seem so, and while holding it, many of them apparently do good work as mental healers. But I wish to show you by contrast, in what respects my own understanding of truth and the way to heal differs from theirs.

I also believe that God is spirit; that he is the only life, truth and love; the only intelligence and substance; and that he fills all space, so that he is everywhere present. I hold, too, that God, through mind, controls all things. But, as to what is termed matter, while I would not quarrel with those who take a different view, I prefer to call it an outward expression of spiritual substance, through which God manifests his omnipotent power. These bodies of ours are the temples of the living God, and constitute with external nature, that continual creation which Christ, the only begotten Son, puts forth from the beginning.

This created being, whom I have already

designated in these letters as the corporeal man, had permission, you will recollect, to enjoy everything that is good; he was innocent and upright so long as he recognized his dependence upon the true source of life. But this corporeal man disobeyed, came to constitute himself the reality and source of power; hence he fell from his state of innocence, and with this sad lapse came discord, disease, death. I do not annul the force of this belief by declaring that sickness, sin, and death have no reality. They are the proofs of a wrong condition of thought on the part of the victim; and show that he has departed out of that state of innocence, that garden of Eden, into which nothing evil can enter. What we call evils, though really such to the thinking of the created or corporeal man, have no effect on the spiritual man, who is Christ; and whenever we become reunited to him, the only life, as the branch is joined to the vine, then we truly live again, and there is no longer any sickness, sin, or death for us; we have passed from death unto life; have lost that self-constituted life in the flesh, and have found the true life, which, if a man have, he shall never die.

While he continues in this fallen condition, man does not understand the true state of the case, or realize his relation to the true vine or source of infinite life. He is like one in a troubled sleep, unconscious of the realities around him, but just enough awake to know that he is under a spell, from which he struggles to get free. In this disturbed dream of the senses evil demons and frightful fancies haunt him, and he tries to awake, and dispel the nightmare that holds him fast. If this sleep overcomes him, he passes into that terrible condition, described in the Bible as being dead in trespasses and sins,—a death from which he will never awake until that resurrection morn, when Christ, the true life, shall quicken again that which remains and is ready to die. And this quickening, when it comes to a man is true healing, and works a thorough reform.

I believe in the terrestrial body of which Paul speaks, on which mind or thought operates, either to purify or defile, according to the moral condition of the man; for "as a man thinketh, so is he." You see, then, that I hold that we have bodies, and are responsible for their safe-keeping; and if we harbor evil and hurtful thoughts, these will surely be reflected some time in some form on the body.

It may be well to say in addition to what is already written, that I do not believe that God is in any way the author or cause of evil. In Adam all died; man is the cause of evil and the only sinner; but with God all is pure, and in Christ are all spiritually made alive. When, therefore, we are, as Paul expresses it, "hid with Christ in God," we shall become new creatures in Christ Jesus, and free from the power of the law of sin and death.

HOW I TREAT.

You ask me to explain to you more fully how I treat disease, and how what you are pleased to call my peculiar theology applies to the healing of the sick. These questions, which are the most difficult of any that bear on the subject, I will try to answer, to the best of my ability. But what I have to say on these points has a direct relation to all that I have written thus far, and will not appear plain to you, unless you keep in mind the main facts in regard to Christ and the condition of the corporeal man, as I have tried to set them forth.

It is true as you observe, that I do not, like those who call themselves "Christian scientists," hold that the body and its diseases are nothing. I accept those facts; but, having done so, I wish to know how such discordant conditions as sickness and suffering came about. Was it by holding pure thoughts? Was it by having our minds stayed on God, who will keep him in perfect peace whose mind is stayed on him? Was it by worshipping the Creator more than the creature? Did these conditions come upon men while they relied solely on Christ, the Lord, as the only source whence they could derive life and power?

The very fact that sickness and pain have become part of the inheritance of mankind shows that the race has departed from that state of true vital union with the source of life in which it was created. Men have turned away from God to trust in an arm of flesh, and wrong thinking and wrong beliefs have brought them into the sad condition in which we now find them. Men came to believe not only that external nature and their own terrestrial life is more real than spirit and spiritual life, but that the source of life and the power to act are in these external expressions of real and absolute being. This led them to forget the spiritual reality which all the while lies back of their individual being, sustaining and enforcing it with power, and to glorify man rather than God, to trust in a material, worldly wisdom more than in that wisdom that is from heaven. Thus man gained the world, but lost his own soul.

Since the fall, man has seemed to be under the curse of a law of sin and death, from which he could see no door of escape, except that of physical death ; and this law which he recognizes and obeys, makes him a servant and a slave. It would seem, then, as if these evils from which men suffer under the law of sin and death did not originate with God, who cannot be the author of evil, but from some other force operating in opposition to God and his government. So strong is this impression fixed in the common mind, that we find that a majority of men believe there is a principle of evil active in the world, as well as a principle of good, and that the two are antagonistic.

But we, who hold that one good and perfect Intelligence created all things that exist, and constituted his holy will the law by which all force acts, must find a way of accounting for what is called evil, without admitting the existence in the universe of an active principle that does not emanate from the one Creator, but is opposed to him. The right view of the case, it seems to me, is to regard what seems to us evil as a perversion of good, and what seems false as a perversion of truth. The sun shines everywhere with intense and steady light; and bathed in that light, all things about us appear as they really are, and assume proper proportions. Yet it is possible to so exclude that light from a given space, a room, for instance, that the objects in that darkened space will seem distorted as we look at them, so that the dim, shadowy outlines of pieces of furniture take the shape of animals, or human forms, or, it may be, of those phantoms of the brain we name ghosts. Just so it is when the mind becomes partially darkened by shutting out the clear light of truth,— objects and relations no longer appear as they really are, but become what our wrong thinking makes them. The truth is not changed on that account; its light is still perfect, and there is nothing but truth; it is only our finite notion of it that has changed; and this apparent change comes about when the real man in us is not in authority, and the earth-born selfhood in us assents its opinion of the condition of affairs. From the standpoint of spirit there is always light, and truth, and harmony; from the standpoint of the bodily senses arise discord and all error.

It is from these limits of selfhood, this law of sin and death to which we are in bondage through fear, that Christ comes to free us. Paul thanked God that he was delivered "from the body of this death," through Jesus Christ, our Lord; and every human being who, weary with struggling against a legion of self-constituted evils, comes to Jesus in the right way, finds rest. When we are willing to be mediums through which truth may shine, instead of champions ready to fight the truth, then the shadows and goblins of night depart, and the full daylight of the sun of righteousness illumines every dark corner of our mental vision.

The all-important starting point for a healer to keep in mind is that true healing comes through Christ and in no other way. "Lord, if thou wilt, thou canst make me clean," expressed the confident belief of a poor sufferer who applied to Jesus; and this is the ground for every healer to take. When we have a confident assurance that Christ is able to make any patient whole, we have taken the first right step.

Having taken the attitude of entire reliance on spiritual power, and abandoned all hope or expectation of being cured in any other way, both healer and patient are prepared to claim the Savior's promise that, if we call upon him in the day of trouble, he will answer us and deliver us. We take our patient in prayer-thought to the very source of healing power, realizing that Christ fully understands the case and is able to supply just what is needed to produce the change desired.

Thus brought face to face with the one perfect life and the power which alone can make perfect; fully realizing that we are not that power, and can do nothing of ourselves to produce the health we seek, we come into a condition of mind to see that our own personal struggles with disease and sin are of no avail; and that even when we strive to conquer the evil in ourselves by bringing some chosen truth to bear upon it, we make no headway.

When at length we perceive that, in all moral cleansing, it is God that worketh in us both to will and to do of his own good pleasure, and realize that it is not for us to combat error with truth, but simply to give up our personal will, and in lowly faith let the spirit of all truth shine and work through us, then, and not till then do we become strong with the strength that Christ supplies. Then alone do we come into an attitude where all the power of the universe of God operates in and through us, producing moral, mental, and bodily health. This condition is truly resting in the Lord, choosing to have his will done rather than our own, and waiting in confident expectation, as did aged Simeon, to see the salvation of God.

It goes without saying that the state of perfect rest and trust herein described enables one to exercise that love which casteth out fear. It is the sweet confidence and repose of a little child in a parent, who, he is sure will take care of him and do what is best for him. Feeling thus, the trustful soul has no farther anxiety, but leaves all issues in the hands of an infinite and loving Father, who is more ready to give good gifts unto his children than they are to receive them. One who attains such a calm state of mind, a mind stayed on God, cannot worry, does not fear, has no solicitude about the issue of his case; for he rests in the Almighty arms, trusts in Infinite wisdom, and knows that whether he live or die, the result will be for the glory of God, and the very best thing that could happen.

Was it not because the condition here indicated, my friend, is the true Christian attitude and spirit, that Jesus so often exhorted those who would enter the kingdom of heaven to become as a little child? And when we enter the presence of that mighty power in which we live, and move, and have our being, what are we but little children, in our ignorance and helplessness? Even the puny will we so foolishly set up against the divine will is a power derived from God. Every remedial agency we make use of for the recovery of the sick owes whatever virtue it may have to the operation of God's direct healing power imparted to it or working through it. The very life to which we cling so fondly, and to preserve which we are ready to make any sacrifice, is the spiritual life flowing through us, and nothing of our own. Nay, we ourselves, what are we but various external expressions of the one life that fills all space?

If this position be the correct one, what are the thoughts with which a healer should regard a patient whom he is called to treat? I have noticed that, in no two cases among those whom the Lord has been pleased to heal through me, has my prayer-thought for them been precisely the same. With one, I seem to plead that he may be brought to Christ and be born again, and realize that he is in the presence of the Savior; another I seem to hold in the prayer that Christ will illuminate his dark mind and thus change the condition of his thought; again, I try to make a patient realize that I have no power to heal or save him, and can only point him to the one savior of all, whom each must accept for himself. These were some of my thoughts, not spoken, of course, only present as a deep, earnest prayer for the patient desiring to be healed. But, after all, it is not an act or a particular thought or prayer that effects the cure; it is the condition of the healer, reflected upon the mind of the patient in such a way as to change his thought.

So far as the bodily effect of treatment is concerned, it is felt, of course, in the mind of the patient. He is operated upon, so to speak, through his thought which is changed. But it is not needful for a healer to have any particular theory about the operation of this subtle mental influence, because it is something independent of his own will, that flows out without his seeking to produce the effect.

The fact that certain persons exert healing

power in a greater degree than others has led many people to regard it as a special gift, possessed in large measure by some persons, and not at all by others. But if the view of Christian healing set forth in these pages be a correct one, the power to work cures is not a gift, in any such sense as the word is here used, but comes to those who are in a proper condition to be good mediums of truth. Nor is the power of healing limited to the use of some particular method or means. All ways are good ways or bad ways, just in proportion as the person who adopts them is guided by the spirit, which alone can cure. But in no case will the patient be made whole if he seeks health for his own selfish advantage, in order that he may continue to gratify the desires of the flesh.

After all, explain this mystery of healing and the regeneration of man as we will, there is still something about it we can never understand, and that baffles our deepest research. I do not know how Jesus wrought the miracles of healing ascribed to him. I do not know how any case of radical cure is produced. Of course, we may say, as the "Christian scientists" do: "God is Spirit. He is the only intelligence, life, and substance in the universe; omnipotent, omniscient, omnipresent. He is perfect, therefore his creation is perfect; and man, made in his own image and likeness, must be a perfect spiritual being, not subject to sickness, sin, and death. These evils, therefore, have no reality, but are delusions and dreams." But does all this formula explain anything, or shed the faintest light on the mystery of healing? I have no doubt that any body may learn to treat disease with success; nor need he know how the effect is produced, in order that it may come to pass. But I also believe that it is impossible for any man to comprehend the process of mental cures, or determine what particular mode of treatment is the best.

WHAT IS REQUIRED OF THE PATIENT.

One of the most difficult things connected with any theory of mental healing is to determine what attitude the patient or subject of healing must take. Many different views on this question are held by successful healers: some assert that it is necessary for the sufferer to exercise faith in the method of mental treatment, and also that he believe in the healer; others, equally sincere, take opposite ground, and declare that it makes no difference with the result of treating whether the recipient have any faith in the means or not. I think, however, that these varying opinions are mainly due to a difference of opinion as to what constitutes a genuine cure. You can readily see that a change in the physical condition that a physician would pronounce a cure is a very different thing from a thorough moral reform which ends in the restoration of the sick patient to bodily health after moral soundness is attained.

"Christian scientists" claim that their treatment reaches beyond a mere bodily cure, and produces a thorough moral transformation, so that the subject of it leads a better life ever after. At the same time there are among those who practise what is called mental or metaphysical healing, who aim in their treatment only to produce a restoration to physical health, and are quite content to withdraw their services when the signs of this outward change appear.

You will perceive from what I have already written, that there are practically two forms of healing, one done on the physical or material plane alone, the other accomplished through the renewing and regeneration of the whole man; and because the first may take place without involving the second, it is important to keep the distinction sharply in mind while discussing what is required of the patient.

WHAT IS REQUIRED OF THE PATIENT. 83

While I should not be satisfied with a healing of bodily disease that went no further, I am willing to grant that such a change may be produced by mental means as well as by medicine, and will, therefore, try to answer your questions about it, before proceeding to explain what to me is the only true and permanent healing wrought through the transforming power of the Christ.

I am well satisfied that there is a natural law of the action of mind upon mind, in accordance with which the thought of one person may be brought so powerfully to bear upon the mind of another as to change his physical condition. We see numerous examples of the operation of this law in every-day life, and can have no reasonable ground for doubt that this personal influence may be powerfully exerted either for good or for ill. The most common instances of it are, perhaps, where one person seeks to control or compel another to a certain course of action against his will. But the same power may be used to promote the welfare of a fellow man.

The explanation of this mental phenomenon is very simple. If we grant what all mental healers claim that diseased bodily conditions are nothing in themselves, but are simply the evidence or outward manifestation of discordant mental states and wrong thinking, it is easy to understand how a person of positive character, who thoroughly believes that right thinking promotes and produces health, may so dominate the mind of a sick person as to inspire in him a like belief. A strong personal will may also aid such a healer in getting the mastery of the mental states of the patient.

You ask how an immoral person may have apparent success in the mental treatment of disease, if healing is really a holy, Christian work. Do you not see that the bodily effects I have just described are not apparently dependent on the moral character of the healer, but are the direct result of certain mental influences of which he has made himself a master? Such a healer applies his mental remedies just as a physician applies his medicines, to bring about certain physical effects; and when this is done his work ceases, because he is not himself in a condition to cure the moral diseases of his patient. People are accustomed to regard the physical change and the disappearance of bodily symptoms as the sure proof that a sick person has recovered, and so do not ask for any other evidence to satisfy them that a mental cure has taken place, and is what it is claimed to be.

I fear that, while they talk a great deal about a higher work and better way of living, many professional mental healers do not, in their own experience, get beyond the plane of the bodily healing just described. This is good as far as it goes, and they who engage in it are not to be despised because they are doing no better; but such cures are not what sin-sick, perishing men most need. The good results are only temporary, and one who has been cured in this way is liable to have a return of the same malady and need curing again.

If mankind were suffering from no deeper ills than the diseases that afflict the body, the kind of healing of which I have spoken would be as good as any other, for it would accomplish all that is desired. Indeed there are many people who do not seem to care for anything beyond their physical comfort, and who consequently prefer just this sort of healing when they are sick, because, while relieving their bodily distress and disability, it does not interfere with the selfish indulgence of their chosen way of life. At the same time, while such healing is better than none, it is only patching a ragged garment, and cannot in the nature of the case be thorough and permanent, because it affects only the external symptoms of disease, but does not reach the cause. Let us therefore consider the other and more radical kind of healing.

What I call true healing begins at the heart and produces a thorough change in the whole man. It is directed to the seat and cause of the trouble, which is the evil that is in thought, which produces the discord of which bodily disease is only the sign.

This higher and broader view of healing is

what the Scriptures designate as the new birth; and if you would grasp my meaning and understanding of the conditions, it will be necessary for you to keep clearly in mind the great foundation truths that I have already explained. We read in the second and third verses of the first chapter of Hebrews Paul's statement that God "hath in these last days spoken unto us by his son, whom he hath appointed heir of all things, by whom also he made the worlds; who being the brightness of his glory, and the express image of his person, and upholding all things by the word of his power, when he had by himself purged our sins, sat down on the right hand of the majesty on high."

In this concise statement of the doctrine of the Christ, Paul declares that the same power that created the worlds, being the express image of God mentioned in the first chapter of Genesis, and the prototype of man, is also the redeemer and savior of the human race, and hath himself purged our sins. There is no true and thorough healing then, as I understand the Scriptures, except that through cleansing and purifying of the heart and life that comes to a man through the acceptance of Christ and the operation of the truth that Christ represents.

What men call bodily disease is the outward sign and expression of the evil within; the radical seat of trouble is the sin-sick soul in man, crying out for the "great physician," longing for the balm in Gilead, asking "What must I do to be saved?"

It is useless and comfortless to offer to such a man a windy theory of the "science of mind," or attempt to relieve his distress by treating the outward symptoms. His trouble is too deep to respond to any superficial remedy. Nothing will *cure* such a case but a power that can save to the uttermost all who apply to him. The words of "mental science" fall upon his ear unheeded; but how eagerly he listens to the voice of Jesus, saying, "Come unto me all ye that labor and are heavy laden, and I will give you rest."

But how are we to offer this potent soul-medicine to the perishing sinner? and what are the indispensable conditions of cure?

I claim that the first step in healing, in every case, is *repentance*. This strong Bible word, so often misunderstood, contains in its very sense the authority for saying that the external or bodily disease is caused by the evil in the heart. A scholar tells me that the word primarily means to punish one's self. When a man *repents* he recognizes the sensations of pain that are the direct result of the evil within him; so that every physical or mental pain which a man feels is an acknowledgment or expression of the deep-seated evil that disturbs his life; and when by the light of truth he brings again into consciousness these pangs or punishments for sin, he *repents*.

The next step is confession. "Confess your faults one to another," says the apostle; and surely a man must confess or admit the facts of his case to himself, or he can never get rid of his sins. This acknowledgment need not be made to a priest or a pastor; but what is essential is a spirit of honesty that does not deny or cover up the truth. It implies that the subject of it is fully aware of his condition, and does not regard it different from what it actually is.

Faith is also required of the patient in order that he may be healed. In James v., 15, we read: "And the prayer of faith shall save the sick and the Lord shall raise him up; and if he have committed sins they shall be forgiven him." Jesus made faith on the part of the applicant a condition of being healed. "Believe ye that I am able to do this?" he asked the blind men; and when they assented he touched their eyes, saying, "According to your *faith* be it unto you." Then to the one who returned to express his gratitude the great Healer said, "Go thy way: thy *faith* hath made thee whole." To one poor woman who sought his healing aid he said, "Thy *faith* hath saved thee: go in peace;" to another, "Daughter, be of good comfort: thy *faith* hath made thee whole."

To be truly, thoroughly healed, a patient must exercise "faith in God," a confidence in his healing power which amounts to a complete surrender of all other hopes, the abandonment of every other means, and utter reliance on Christ. It implies a readiness to forsake every evil thought or desire that stands in the way of recovery, and a belief that the cure sought may immediately take place. In such a state of mind the patient may pray for healing mercy; others may pray for him that he may be healed; and his sins may be forgiven. The Scribes, you will recollect, were sorely offended because Jesus, when healing a man sick of the palsy, changed the formula "arise and walk," to "Be of good cheer: thy sins are forgiven thee."

No truth in the Bible is more plainly taught than this, that healing begins and ends with the forgiveness and cure of sin. Here is the prime cause and seat of the trouble, and no treatment is complete which fails to destroy the germ of the disease, and cleanse that which is within as well as what is external. "Woe unto you who make clean the outside!" declared Jesus, "but do nothing to eradicate the germs of evil hidden within." First cleanse the fountain; then will all the streams become sweet and wholesome.

Note too, that Christ is constantly warning his disciples and followers not to mistake any form of superficial and partial cure for true and thorough healing: "Strive to enter in at the straight gate; for many, I say unto you, shall seek to enter in and shall not be able." "I am the way, the truth, and the life." "I am the door of the sheepfold." "No man cometh unto the father but by me." "If the truth make you free, ye shall be free indeed." "I am come to seek and to save that which was lost." "There is joy in heaven over one sinner that repenteth." "He that forsaketh not all that he hath and followeth me cannot be my disciple." "Many will say unto me in that day, Lord, Lord, have we not prophesied in thy name, and in thy name cast out devils, and in thy name done many wonderful works? Then will I profess unto them, I never knew you." "My disciples are they who do the will of my Father, which is in heaven."

You perceive that according to the view

herein presented, Christian healing and saving faith are one and the same thing. For this reason the burden of the gospel message to sick and fallen men is Faith. "Whatsoever is not of faith is sin."— Romans xiv., 23. "But before faith came, we were kept under the law, shut up under the faith which should afterwards be revealed."— Gallatians iii., 23. "For whatsoever is born of God overcometh the world: and this is the victory that overcometh the world, even our faith."— I John v., 4.

Having now explained as clearly as possible my own idea of what in the Bible is meant by true healing, a simple exercise of genuine *repentance* and *faith*, I see no necessity to further burden you with any of the theories with which teachers of what is called mental healing are apt to confuse the learner and mislead him in his search after truth. The first form of healing to which I have alluded in this letter is not the kind I approve; therefore I do not trouble myself or you with any theories about it. Take it for what it is worth, but do not neglect the better way. The door to eternal life is not barred against any repentant, humble seeker for admission. No knowledge of any theories of mind or matter is required to enter. "If thou wouldst enter into life keep the commandments." A knowledge of "Christian science," or any other science, is not necessary in order to be saved with a salvation that redeems man from the power and dominion of the law of sin and death, and makes him a child of God, a free-born heir to truth and all of the truth. Repentance, confession, forsaking sin, prayer, faith, lowly obedience to the teachings of the Holy Spirit,—these are the steps in the true healing process, and constitute the only doctrines or lessons that any one needs to learn, in order to recover from illness, enjoy the blessing of perfect health, and enter into that heaven of reality from which all sin, suffering and death are forever banished, and all the children of God are one with the Father and with his only begotten Son, Jesus Christ, our Savior.

GEMS BY G. F. CHAPMAN.

The teaching most needed to-day, is that which teaches man to lose his self-life, and thereby gain eternal life.

Teach me how to abide in the Vine, then shall I become a powerful instrument of divine healing.

Teach man to remove the beam from his own eye, then can he see clearly, to remove the mote from his brother's eye.

You would not judge the beauty of a rose, before it was unfolded. Neither should you judge man's life and character until it is unfolded.

Are you not trying to get outside of God to find him?

Spiritual understanding is not gained through struggling, but by acceptance.

Do not exhaust all your time in asking, but devote some to accepting and gratitude.

Humility is the stepping-stone to perfection.

Perfect love does not excite, but fills with emotion.

Our nearest and most dangerous neighbor is Self.

From discord to harmony is not a rapid transit.

You cannot lose Self, except in the knowledge of eternal life.

Mental darkness is not the absence of light but the lack of comprehension.

God deserves more than constant petitions; He deserves praise.

God is not a present help until we are ready to accept his free gift.

Soul and body healing is but the comprehension of our life source.

When we are abiding in the Vine, we are only hid from the man of sense, not from spirit.

If we are abiding in the Vine, why need we trouble about the fruit we are to bear? Certainly the branch cannot bear other than the natural fruit.

Argument will never convert the world; truth lived and demonstrated only can.

GEMS BY LAILA E. CHAPMAN.

Age 16 years.

Self-conceit will lead man astray.

Vanity is no part of a Christian.

Heavenly riches should be desired rather than worldly.

Human mind is not vast enough to comprehend all truth at once.

As the rose opens gradually to the sunlight, so truth comes to them that search for it.

Pen cannot portray nor words express the thoughts of a thinking man.

Bigotry is a stumbling-block, on the way to the kingdom.

>Love is the corner-stone,
>That will always stand,
>On which is chiselled
>   The way to the throne
>By God's own hand.

QUESTIONS.

Did it ever occur to you, that dominion was not given to earth man, but to the spiritual man (Christ) who was truth and life?

What has dominion over the fowls of the air, fish of the sea, and every creeping thing, except truth and life?

Jacob claimed to have seen God face to face: yet John declared that no man hath seen God at any time, but did you ever realize that the man with whom Jacob wrestled was this man in the first creation, who is the Lord God, hence he saw the (Only Begotten) Son?

Did it ever occur to you that those who half believe are the only ones who argue the problem of spiritual life? because he who has come to the knowledge of the truth fully realizes that he cannot prove by controversy the evidence within of immortality.

Do you know that your condition is either what you make it or what you allow God to make it? The preference is yours. Whom will you serve? Self or God?

MR. G. F. CHAPMAN,
MRS. M. E. CHAPMAN,

TEACHERS OF THE

Gospel of Christian Healing,

No. 17 Howard Street, Malden, Mass.

Classes formed monthly, beginning September 1, 1888.

Since the object of this instruction is not the mere art of physical healing, but the reformation that results in godly living, such only as desire the latter are invited to join the classes.

The aim in these courses of lessons is, first, to lead students to turn from sin and death to holiness and life; second, to explain how they may live in health and peace, and above the world; third, to unfold the true meaning and purpose of prayer, especially the prayer of faith that will save the sick.

☞ Mr. and Mrs. Chapman have in preparation a text-book, in which their methods and course of instruction are fully set forth and explained. The book will be ready in time for the use of classes.

☞ Mrs. Chapman has a private class out of the State during the month of May, and will open another at her residence, in June.

Deacidified using the Bookkeeper process
Neutralizing agent Magnesium Oxide
Treatment Date April 2006

PreservationTechnologie
A WORLD LEADER IN PAPER PRESERVATIC
111 Thomson Park Drive
Cranberry Township, PA 16066
(724) 779 2111

CPSIA information can be obtained
at www.ICGtesting.com
Printed in the USA
LVHW082343301022
731945LV00003B/19